CaChoo It!

by Chaia M May

Publisher, Editorial, Sales and Customer Service Office

LearningPlay LLC

Menlo Park, CA 94025

Copyright © 2014-6

All rights reserved. No part of the material protected by this copyright notice may be reproduced or utilized in any form, electronic or mechanical, including photocopying, recording, or by any information storage and retrieval system, without written permission from the copyright owner.

All rights preserved with the purchased and free art work used in this publication.

Library of Congress Cataloging-in-Publication Data

May, Chaia M., 1959 -

    Illustrated Children Books:

    ISBN 978-0-9864121-6-5

    1. Illustrated Children Books, May

Kudos

Ami, Dionne, Donald, Lili, Peter and Rose

Happy Heart CaChoo!

Introduction

When children are struggling with anything, particularly an instrument, they forget that learning can be fun. They need to be reminded that they are "playing," not "working" an instrument!

A **CaChoo** is a fun symbol of accomplishment, no more than a line drawn by a child on a page* with a flourish. We exuberantly exclaim "CaChoo!" in order to inspire him or her to practice and to "do it again" until the material is mastered. Mastery can be an abstract concept but the "CaChoo method" makes it concrete: the children know they have to "get" it on their own and eventually play it with no mistakes.

If the piece is challenging, I say a child can get a CaChoo after playing it correctly three times in a row. That's because after three times, our hands revert to automatic and we need to direct our hands with our 'minds' by telling our hands out loud what to do. The beauty of a CaChoo is that it is so simple. It comes from the child, with only the go-ahead from the teacher. This allows for open ended creativity on the child's part to make it truly his or her own. By using a CaChoo even the youngest children can express their uniqueness with their own "signature" without needing to know how to write.

I use CaChoos for teaching music but they apply to any subject! The CaChoos are small enough so that they allow the children to still be able to read the material on the page while leaving a proud track of their achievements.

I have been utterly delighted at what imaginative variations children have come up with and how they have owned "the concept of CaChooing" so easily. What is more satisfying than crossing off an item on your list? Here we do it with flair! Not to mention pride, joy, and applause. CaChooing has helped the children replace their self-doubt with confidence and push them beyond just "getting by" with a willingness to polish their work as if they were a diamond!

No longer do we have to explain what mastery is. We just do it and **CaChoo It!**

Sincerely,
Chaia

* Should the child or the teacher want to preserve the book or material on the page, you can make it smaller and put it on a post-it note so not to deface the book.

Contents

"Perfect" versus "Mistake" School   6

What is a CaChoo?   7

Dealing with Mistakes:
A Mistake versus 'What You Don't Know'   8
See a Mistake as an Open Door!   10
Say "Hip-Hip Hurray" to Mistakes!   12

General Techniques:
Baby Steps   14
Stre - - e - - tch Yourself — Talent Grows!   16
Brain Freeze!   18
Put Your Brain in Your Hands!   20
Other Hand Appreciation Day   22

Thoughts and Feelings:
Things That Get in the Way—Thoughts and Feelings   24
Let it Rain Feelings   26
Let Your Scary Feelings In—Don't Stop Them!   28
"New" Rather than "Hard"   30
Trying Vs. Doing & Coin Game   32-33
Be In Your Own Movie!   34
You Do a CaChoo & Thinking vs. Doing   36-37
Working on Playing-Playing at Learning?   38

"Perfect" versus "Mistake" School

The sign on the door to my music studio says:

If you need to be perfect, you are at the wrong school—
If you make mistakes, this IS the right place
and you are welcome!

What is a CaChoo?

So, what is a CaChoo?
First you draw a line.
Then you make it into anything you want it to be.

A CaChoo on a page of your music book is a way to say you did a great job. It can be a small mark in the corner or a big one across the page. It is anything to show that you know how to play that song well and only need to play it again to enjoy it.

You will make many mistakes along the way to learning. The CaChoo is a reward for getting through and learning from these mistakes. I hope what you find in this book will help you see that making mistakes is O.K. Know that if you take on a bigger challenge, more mistakes are likely to happen. It is then easier to take the mistakes in stride. When you look back at all those CaChoos you made, I know you will be proud and amazed at what you were able to accomplish

What you see in this book are some of the CaChoos that my students created from their imagination once they learned the assigned song. Please send me any CaChoos that you have drawn so I can share and delight in your success!

Chaia

A Mistake versus 'What You Don't Know'

If everyone makes mistakes, then how can they be 'BAD?'

Change your words to: "I'm finding out what I don't know."

Try closing your eyes when you play your song.
You'll find out what your hands know and do not know.

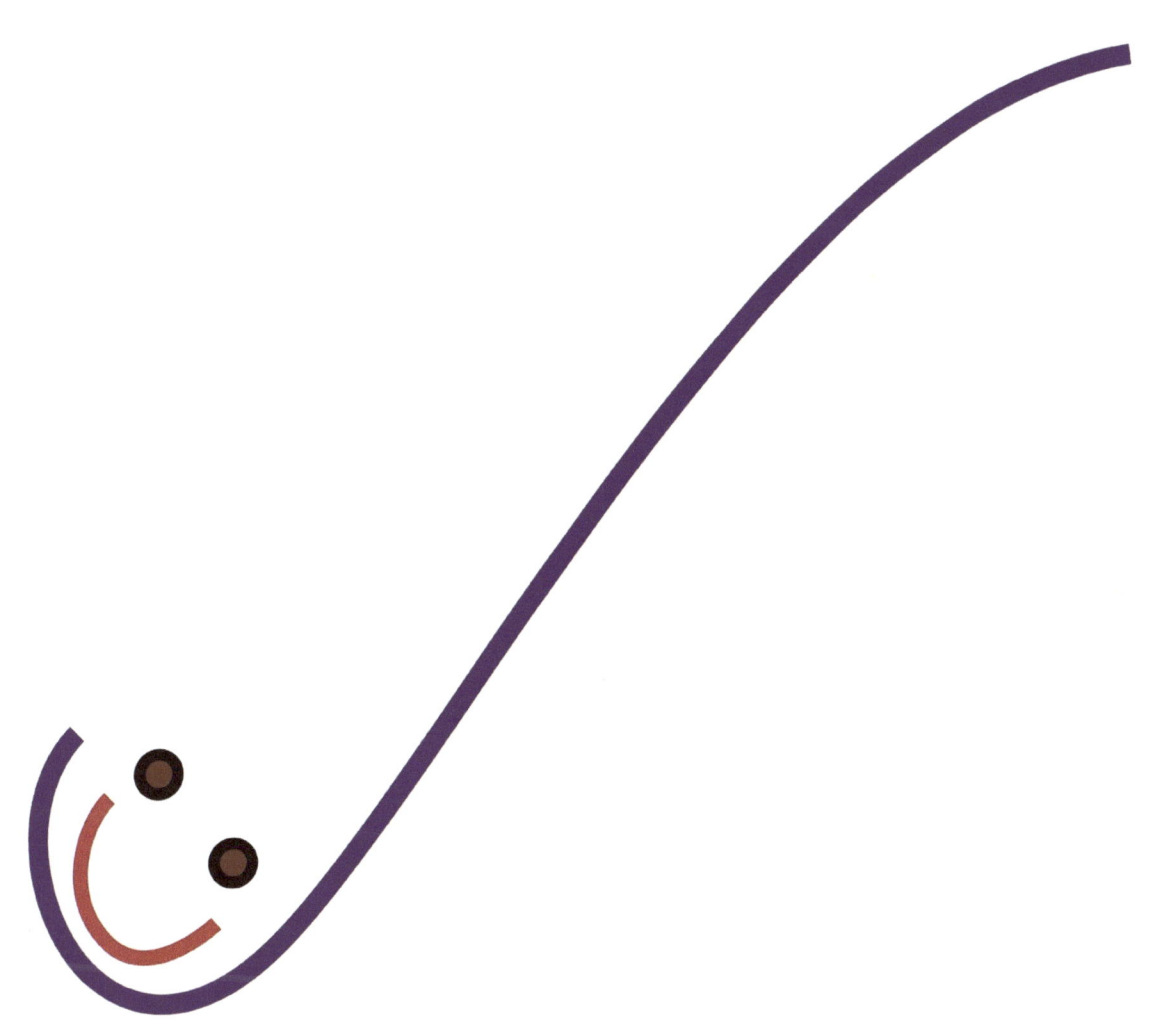

Happy CaChoo!

See a Mistake as an Open Door!

When you make a mistake say,

"I'm going through a new door."

It's O.K. not to know what's on the other side!

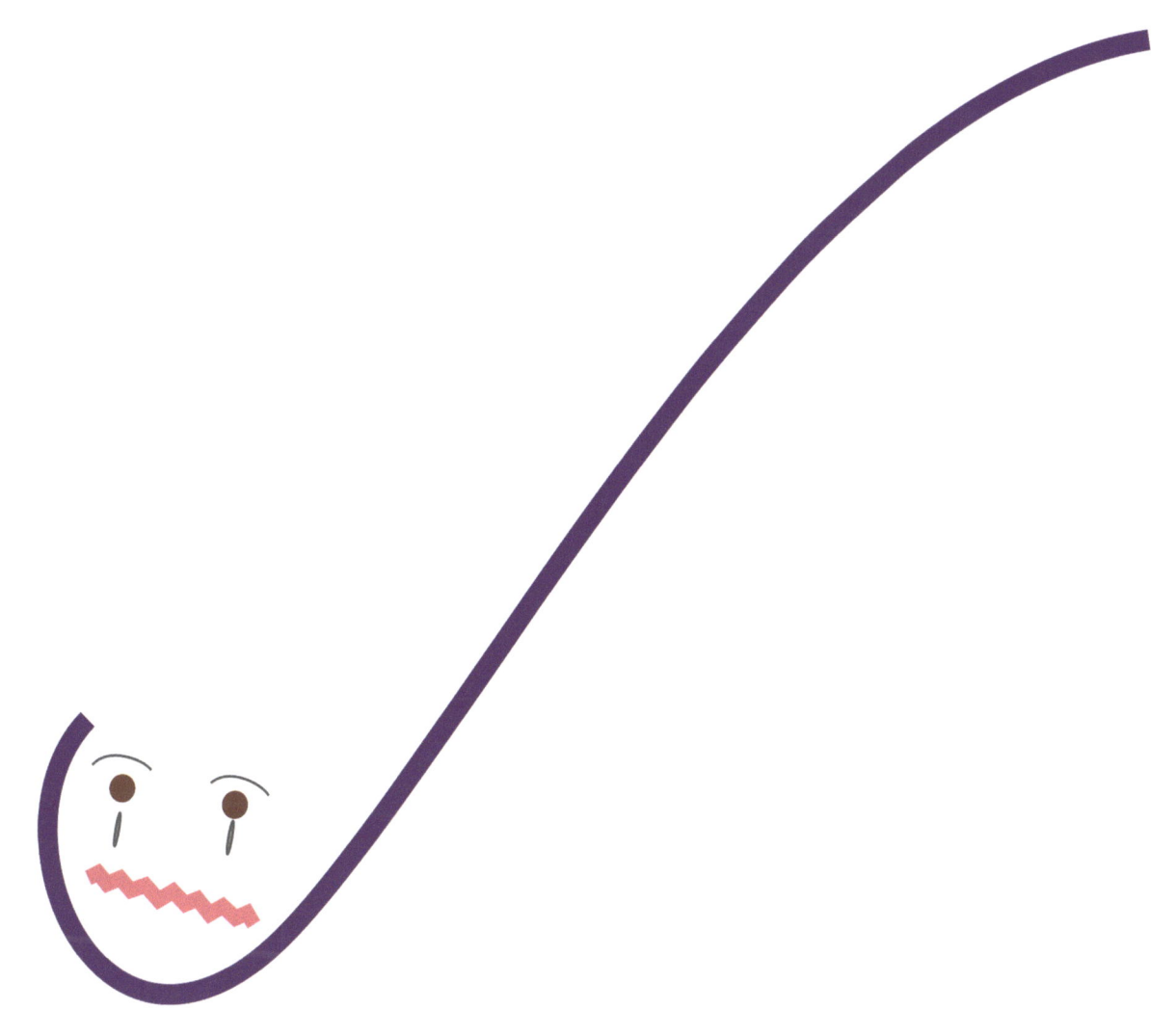

BooHoo CaChoo!

Say "Hip Hip Hurray" to Mistakes!

When you make a mistake, say, "Hip Hip HURRAY!"

When you are fixing a mistake is when you are learning the most, so celebrate !

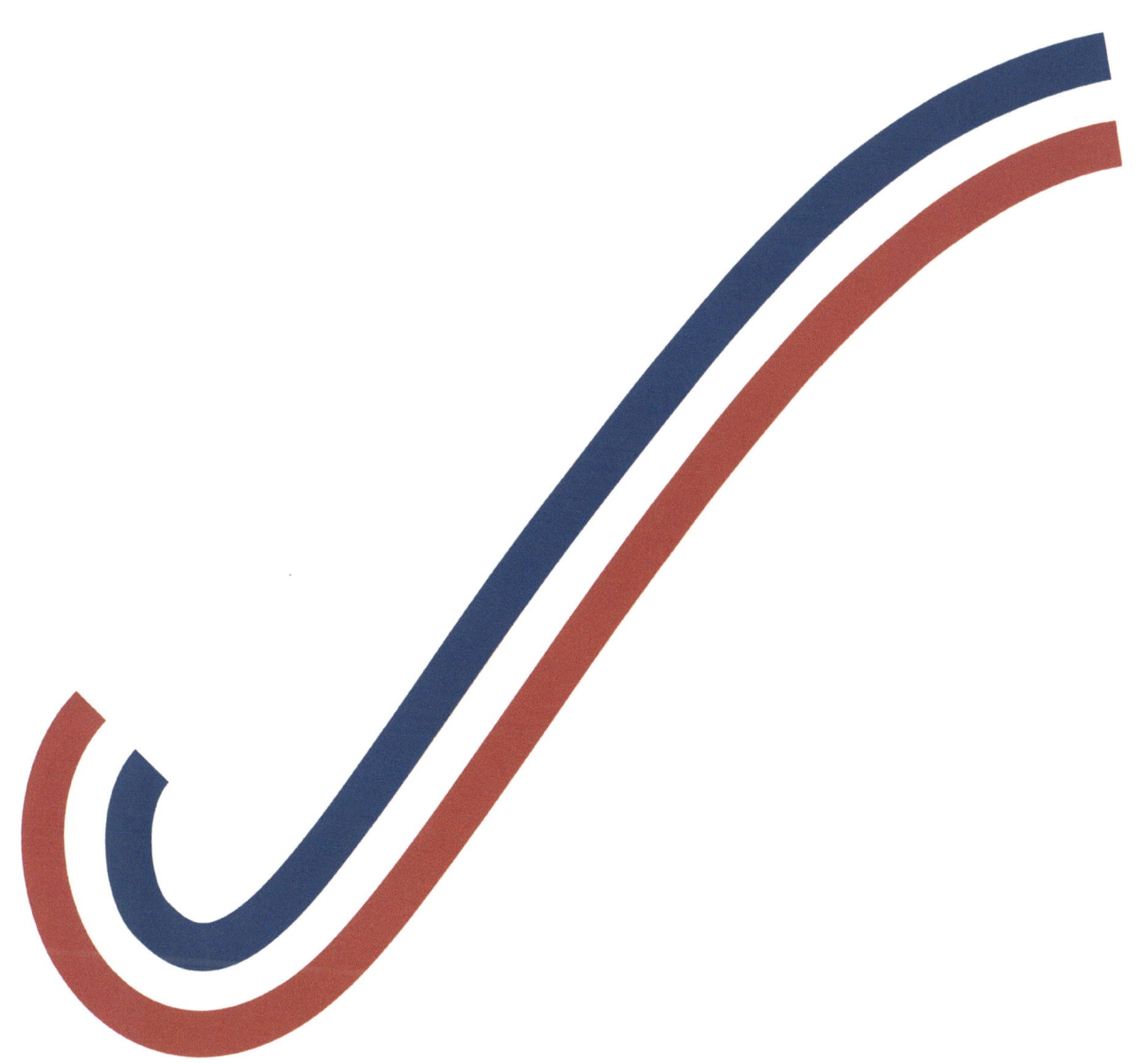

Celebrate Red-White-Blue CaChoo!

Baby Steps

You can do most anything if you break it down into smaller steps.

You learned to walk that way!
You can learn to play that way!

Trick yourself—cover the notes of the song except for the first measure.
Once you've got it, uncover just the next measure!

Baby Steps CaChoo!

Stre - - e - - tch Yourself — Talent Grows!

Both skills and abilities will grow when you practice challenging pieces.

When you practice "well," you always get better! Practice is never a waste of time because you always come home from "The Practice Store" with something in your hands.

Mini-Tipping Point Game

With each first try, imagine "taping" what you learned on it; the second time, "gluing" it on; the third time "painting" it on with permanent paint. At that point we say it, "gets under your skin" or it becomes part of you.

Stretch CaChoo!

Brain Freeze!

Trying too hard can shut down our brains.

You can trick your brain by playing the left hand part with the right hand and vice versa.

Brain Freeze CaChoo!

Put Your Brain in Your Hands!

The muscles in your hands remember what they were doing and will do what they have been trained to do. Since your hands are good at what they just learned, you don't need to call it a mistake when they don't "obey" you right away on a new piece.

Tell your hands what to do by saying the notes out loud. Then once they get it, your "brain is in your hands" and you don't need to think about it anymore.

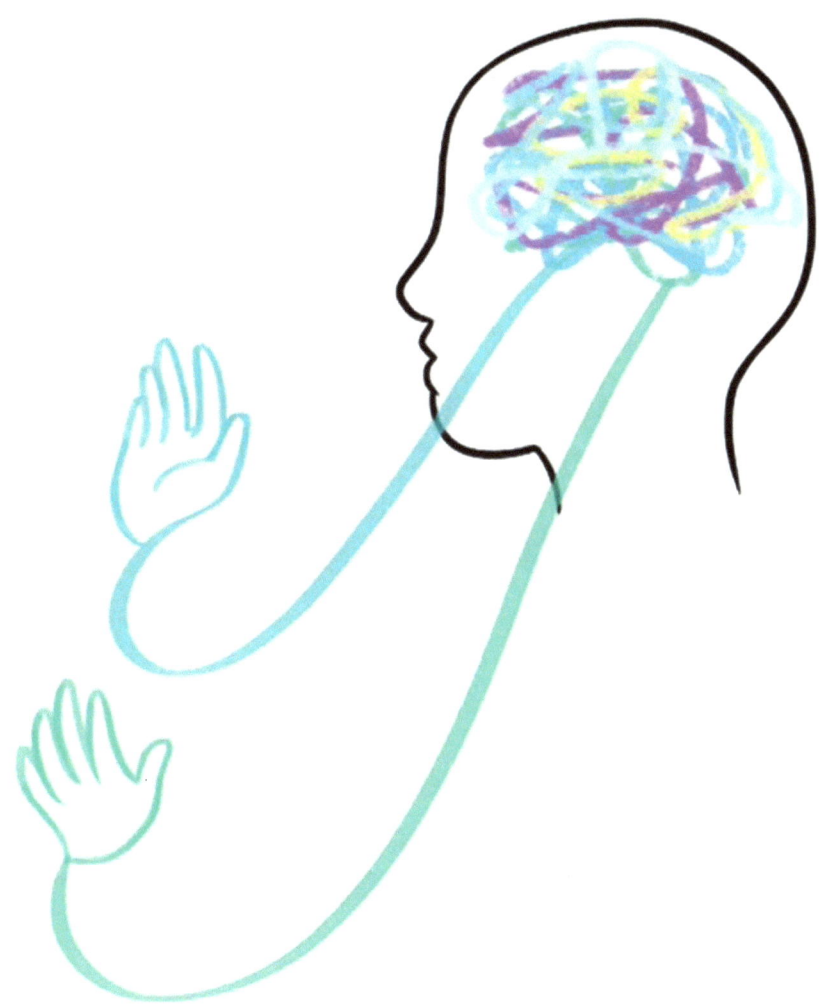

Brain in Hands CaChoo!

Other Hand Appreciation Day

It is impossible that one hand is less 'smart' than the other.

Yet, many will call their weaker hand, "Stupid." Weaker hands just need a bit more practice. Give the weaker hand more time—it will then show you how much "smarter" it is!

Hand it to You CaChoo

Things That Get in the Way—Thoughts and Feelings

It is amazing!

Thousand's of thoughts go through your mind every day.

Trying not to think about something sometimes makes you think about it more rather than less!

Listening to every thought, you might not stay on the task at hand.

Your thoughts don't have to get you off track. Try just watching them go by like a piece of wood floating down a river.

In a moment,

it will float away.

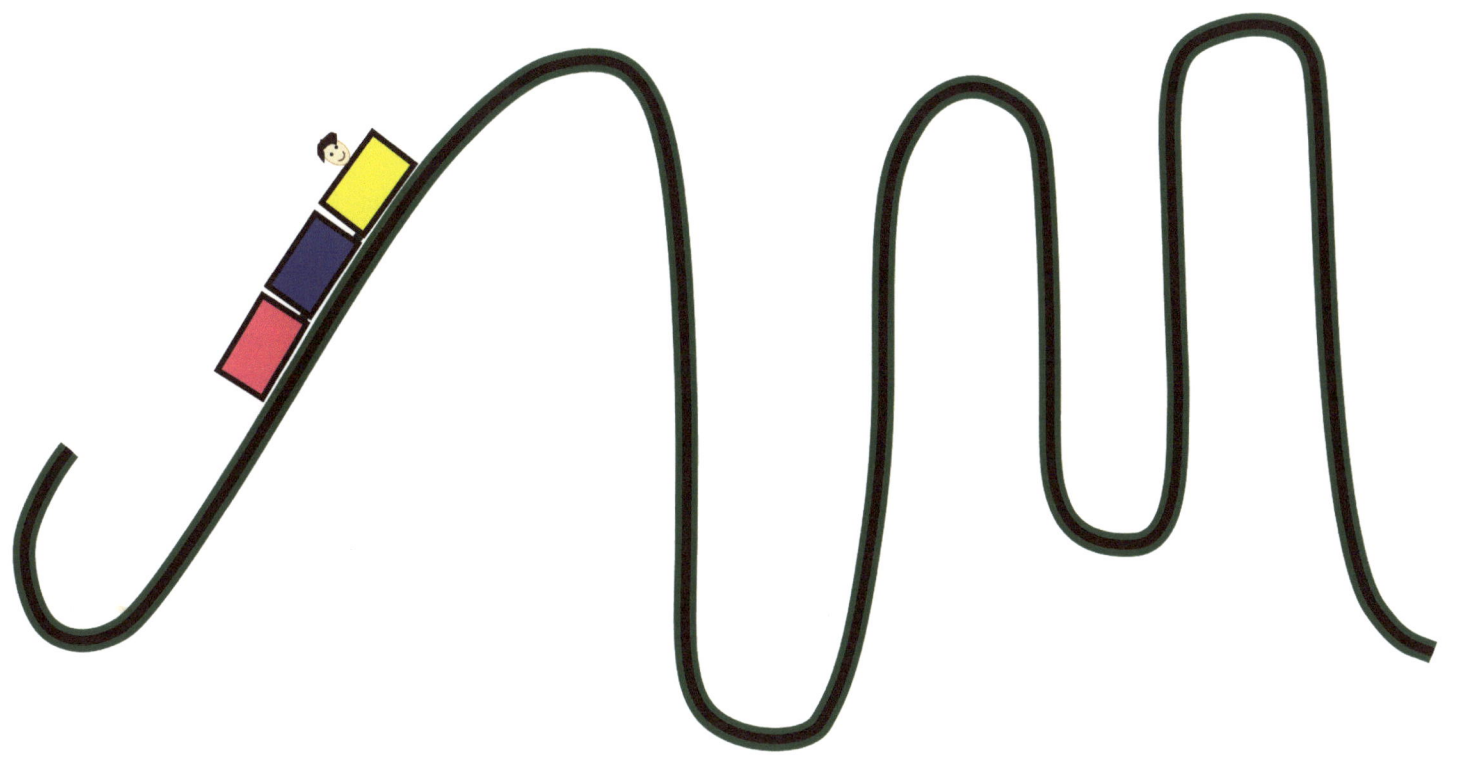

Roller Coaster CaChoo

Let it Rain Feelings

When we try something new, sometimes we get mad when it doesn't come easily.

Anger can be like an umbrella. It can open up to protect us from other feelings that are "raining down on us."

While that umbrella is up we don't have to feel the feelings and we can hide under it.

Or, we can come out from under the umbrella for a minute and "get wet" with feelings we don't want to feel and know that soon
we will be dry and be just fine.

Rainy Day CaChoo

Invite Your Scary Feelings In — Don't Stop Them!

If an upsetting feeling comes "in" like a wave, imagine you are a surfer and welcome the wave. "Ride" the feeling and see how it will carry you for only a moment and then go away.

- - - -

Pretend you are erasing fearful thoughts with a Giant Eraser! Then the thoughts cannot give you the feeling that what you are about to do is scary.

That way you can start each task with a clean white sheet.

How does your head know what your hands can do before they do it?

Anything is possible because the future has not happened yet, right?!

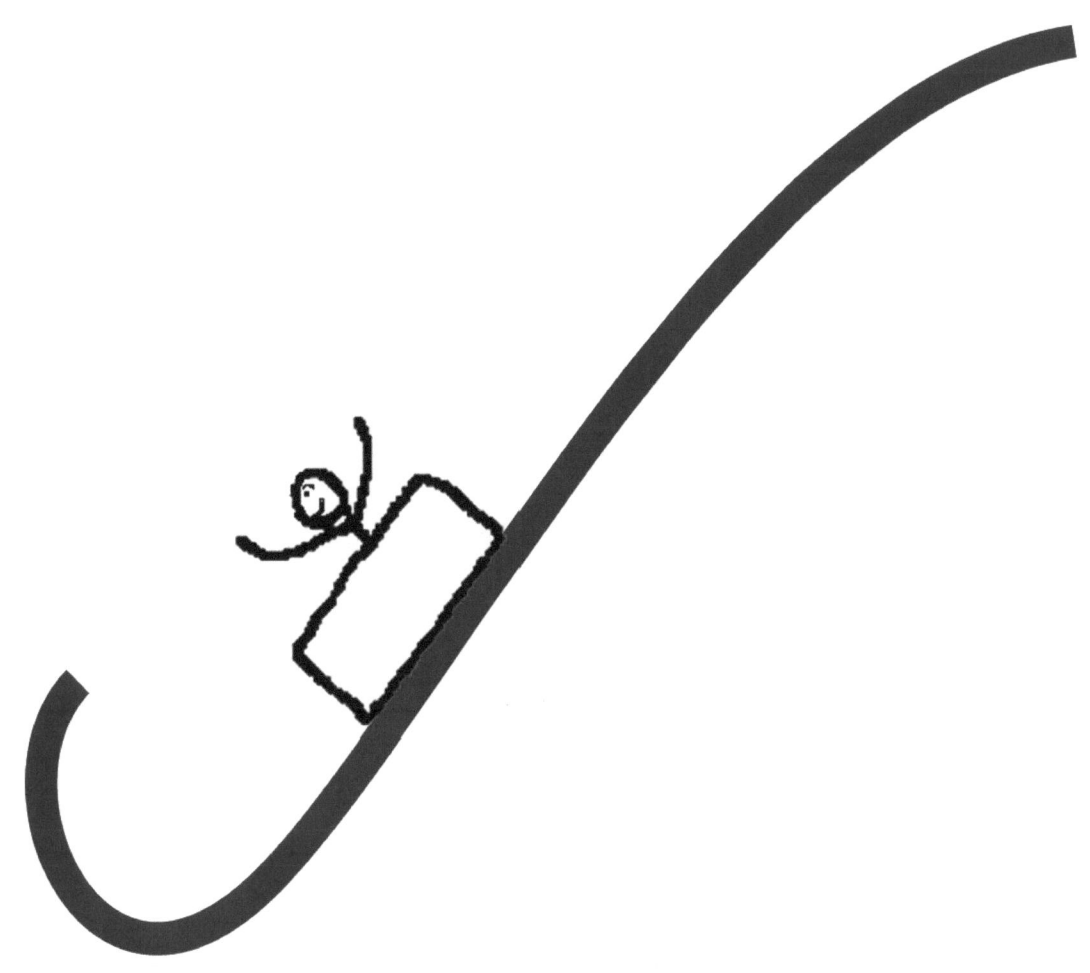

"Eraser Surfboard" CaChoo!

"New" Rather than "Hard"

"Hard" often means you think you have to do it right the first time. You may feel like you are climbing a tall mountain and might fall down. However, when you learn to play an instrument, you can't fall down so you won't get 'hurt' doing this 'new' challenge.

You can say what you are doing is "new" rather than saying it is "hard." Then, all you know is that you don't know it ... yet!

Take off the pressure by assuming it will take you one hundred times to get it right. Then if you do it in fewer tries, you will feel great!

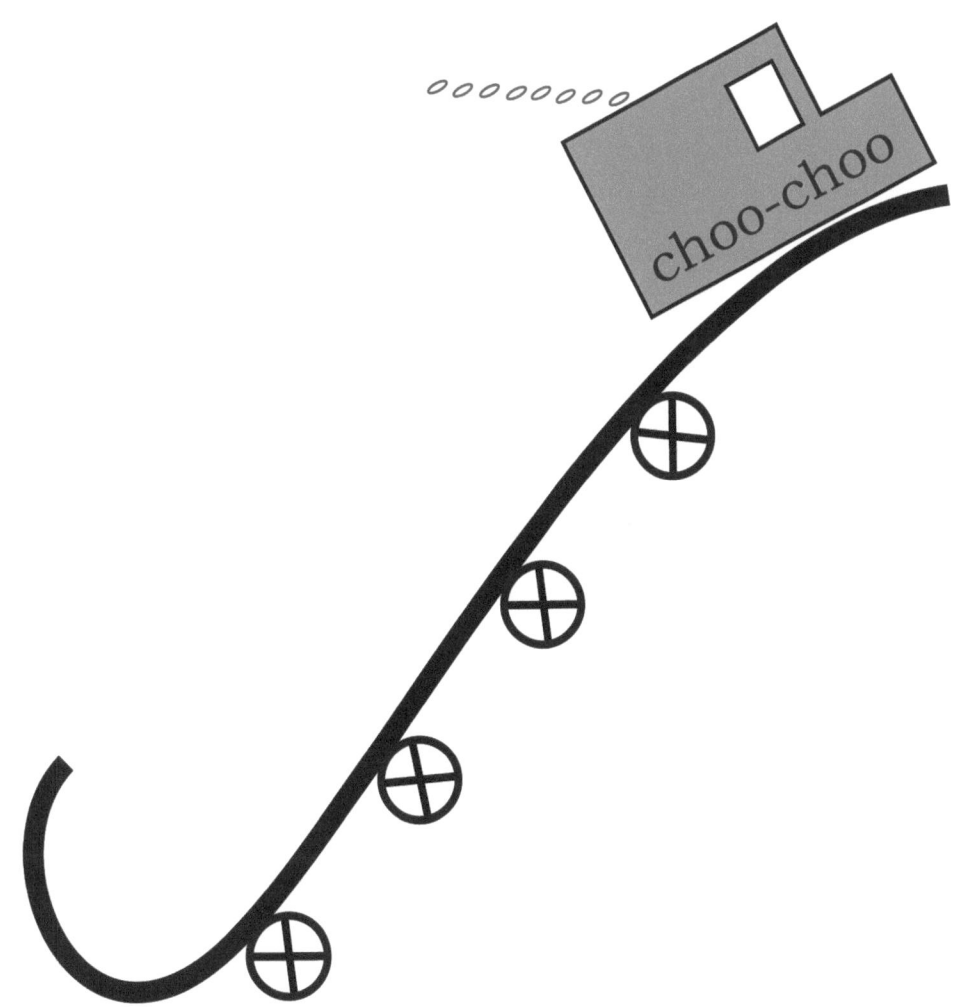

Choo-Choo CaChoo!

Trying versus Doing

Trying puts you in the past or the future.
Doing puts you in the present!

Saying "I'll try" means that you are either remembering that you have failed in the past or you might not succeed in the future.

Why not just say "I am doing it" and imagine yourself doing it correctly.

Once you get going, it won't feel hard because you will be in the "flow" and it will feel easier.

Coin Game

Your parents pay for lessons and work to earn that money. Your job is to get the most out of each lesson. So, put seven coins by the side of a jar at each lesson. When you practice each day, put a coin in.

At the end of the week, you will have kept the value of your efforts during the lesson and added to the value by practicing and getting even better!

Then your parents can even choose to put seven more coins into the jar to add to your seven coins. Together you can choose an appropriate reward!

Be In Your Own Movie!

Imagine you are the star of your own movie.
If you compare yourself to someone else, it is like you are walking off the screen to be in the other person's movie.
That means there is no one left in your own show!

Be the star you are, as unique as the stars in the sky!

Focus on what you can do,
rather than what everyone else is doing!

You CaChoo!

You Do a CaChoo

Thinking vs. Doing

If you think the water in a swimming pool is cold, it will be "hard" to just jump in.

If you just jump in, it will be much easier.

Thinking about a musical piece as "hard" prevents you from making that jump.

Jump in! See how the "scary" feeling goes away and you become "fear-less" as you find it gets easier.

Working on Playing—Playing at Learning?

We say "play" an instrument—not "work" an instrument.

While you are "working on playing" something new, you are always "playing" the piano. Life can be seen as work or play, so why not see learning as a fun game?

Do your "home play," rather than "home work!"

Know that you can enjoy what you are doing anytime in the game and don't have to wait until you master the piece.

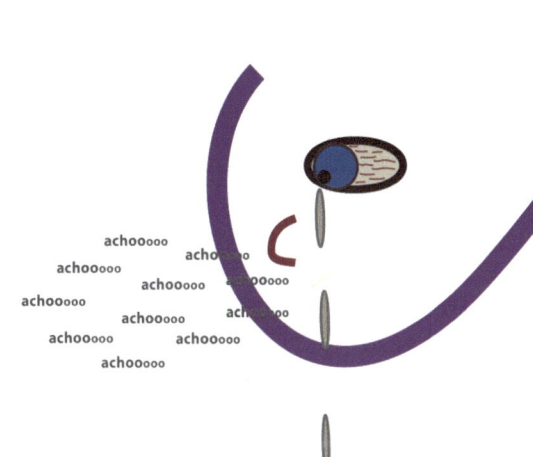

Achoo! CaChoo

Silly Spellings of CaChoo

CuChoo

KuChoo

KaChoo

QueChoo

KeChoo

KooChoo

KoChoo

CooChoo

ChooCa! (backwards)

Can you add more Silly CaChoos?

The Author

Chaia May has been an educator since 1986, focusing on helping children find and express their innate abilities particularly in the arts. She runs a music studio in the Bay Area, offering classes in piano, guitar, voice and general early childhood music education. She has a strong interest in helping those of all ages who learn differently, inspired by her earlier challenges as a parent.

Her degrees are from Wellesley College (BA in Political Science/Anthropology) and Stanford University (MA in Applied Communication Theory/ Children's Media Development.) She has received director level credits from Foothill College in Early Childhood Administration and taken many post M.A. classes in Education.

Chaia has written twelve books on Early Childhood Jewish Education, including original stories for children to teach ethics, manners and spiritual awareness. She has lectured around the country on the Neurological Basis of Prayer and applying Sensory Integration to Early Childhood Classroom Curriculum. A new story-based math series for children is being launched as well!

Chaia's other accomplishments include a musical fable for children to teach empathy, a curriculum to teach Classical Music for Young Families as part of her Classical Music Institoot!, and her two beautiful, independent daughters Hannah, and Ami.

www.ingramcontent.com/pod-product-compliance
Lightning Source LLC
Chambersburg PA
CBHW041536040426
42446CB00002B/108